Nita Mehta's
Different ways with
Vegetables

Nita Mehta

B.Sc. (Home Science), M.Sc. (Food and Nutrition), Gold Medalist

Tanya Mehta

SNAB

Publishers Pvt Ltd

Nita Mehta's
Different ways with
Vegetables

© Copyright 2003-2006 **SNAB** Publishers Pvt Ltd

3rd Print 2006
ISBN 81-7869-042-x

Food Styling and Photography: **SNAB**

Layout and laser typesetting :

National Information
Technology Academy
3A/3, Asaf Ali Road
New Delhi-110002
☎ 23252948

Published by :

SNAB
Publishers Pvt. Ltd.
3A/3 Asaf Ali Road,
New Delhi - 110002
Tel: 23252948, 23250091
Telefax:91-11-23250091

Editorial and Marketing office:
E-159, Greater Kailash-II, N.Delhi-48
Fax: 91-11-29225218, 29229558
Tel: 91-11-29214011, 29218727, 29218574
E-Mail: nitamehta@email.com
nitamehta@nitamehta.com
Website: http://www.nitamehta.com
Website: http://www.snabindia.com

Distributed by :

THE VARIETY BOOK DEPOT
A.V.G. Bhavan, M 3 Con Circus,
New Delhi - 110 001
Tel : 23417175, 23412567; Fax : 23415335
Email: varietybookdepot@rediffmail.com

Printed by :

STANDARD PRESS (INDIA) PVT. LTD.

Rs. 89/-

About The Recipes

What's In A Cup?

INDIAN CUP
1 teacup = 200 ml liquid
AMERICAN CUP
1 cup = 240 ml liquid (8 oz.)

The recipes in this book were tested with the Indian teacup which holds 200 ml liquid.

Introduction

$\mathcal{V}$ariety is the spice of life! Prepare your favourite vegetable in many different ways - using different spices and different combinations, thus creating totally new and delicious subzis.

Vegetables make an invaluable contribution towards the **supply of minerals and vitamins and they are also low in calories**. They are rich in fibre, add bulk to the diet and assist in digestion. Every meal should include a vegetable, which may be a main dish or an accompaniment to the main dish. Delicious curries, koftas, bhujias and semi-dry masala preparations give variety to meals. ***Baingan ka Saalan, Broccoli Koftas, Kachumber Gobhi, Hyderabadi Bhindi*** and such many other delicacies will make your family wanting more.

Nita Mehta

CONTENTS

Bhindi
(LADY'S FINGER)

Kurkuri Ajwaini Bhindi   34
Achaari Bhindi   36

Matar
(PEAS)

Matar Dhania Wale   38
Kastoori Gajar Matar   40

Arbi
(COLOCASIA)

Karaari Bharwaan Arbi   42
Arbi Ajwaini   44

Gajar
(CARROT)

Kofte Gajar Ke   46
Gajar Methi   48

Khumb
(MUSHROOM)

Makki Matar Khumb   50
Bharwaan Khumb Curry   52
Mushroom Chettinad   54
Khumb Nadiyaan Kinare   58

Baingan
(BRINJAL)

Baingan Mirch Ka Saalan   60
Chutney Waale Bharwaan Baingan   62
Hyderabadi Baingan   64

Anjeeri Gobhi

Fried cauliflower, cooked in an anjeer flavoured masala.

Picture on back cover   *Serves 6*

1 medium cauliflower (gobhi) - cut into medium size florets with long stalks
1 tsp jeera (cumin seeds)
2 onions - chopped
1 tsp chopped ginger
1 tsp chopped garlic
2 green chillies - deseeded & chopped

ANJEER PASTE
8 small anjeers (figs)
1 cup dahi (yogurt)
1 tsp garam masala
¾ tsp red chilli powder
1¾ tsp salt or to taste

TO SPRINKLE
2 small anjeers (figs) - chopped and roasted on a tawa (griddle)

1. Break the cauliflower into medium florets, keeping the stalk intact.
2. Heat 1 cup oil in a kadhai. Add all the cauliflower pieces and fry to a golden colour. Remove from oil and keep aside.
3. Churn all the ingredients given under anjeer paste in a mixer till smooth.
4. Heat 2 tbsp oil in a kadhai. Add jeera. When it turns golden, add chopped onions. Stir till light brown.
5. Add ginger, garlic and green chillies. Cook for a minute.
6. Add the prepared anjeer paste. Stir-fry for 2-3 minutes till the curd dries up a little. Keep aside till serving time.

Step 7

7. Chop finely 2 anjeers and roast on a tawa till fragrant. Keep aside.
8. At serving time, heat the masala and add fried cauliflower. Mix well.
   Serve hot, sprinkled with roasted pieces of anjeer.

Phool Dilkhush

Pan fried whole cauliflowers coated with a masala and topped with green peas.

Picture on page 29   *Serves 4*

2 very small whole cauliflowers
4 tbsp oil, 3 onions - ground to a paste
3 tomatoes - roughly chopped, 1" piece ginger - chopped
seeds of 1 moti illaichi, 3-4 saboot kali mirch (peppercorns) and 2 laung (cloves)
2 tbsp curd - beat well till smooth
½ tsp red chilli powder, ½ tsp garam masala, ½ tsp haldi, ½ tsp amchoor
½ tsp salt, or to taste, ¼ cup boiled peas (matar) - to garnish

1. Remove stems of cauliflowers. Boil 6 cups water with 2 tsp salt. Put the whole cauliflowers in it. When the water starts to boil again, remove from fire. Leave them in hot water for 10 minutes. Remove from water and refresh in cold water. Wipe dry on a clean kitchen towel.

2. Heat 5-6 tbsp oil in a large flat kadhai or a pan. Put both cauliflowers with flower side down in oil. Cover and cook on medium flame, stirring occasionally till the cauliflowers turn golden and get patches of dark

brown colour here and there. Remove from oil. Keep aside.

3. Heat ½ tbsp oil in a clean kadhai. Add moti illaichi, saboot kali mirch and laung. After a minute add chopped tomatoes & ginger. Cook for 4-5 minutes till they turn soft. Grind the cooked tomatoes to a paste.

4. Heat 3½ tbsp oil. Add onion paste. Cook till onions turn golden brown.

5. Add tomato paste, cook for 4 minutes on low flame till it turns dry.

6. Add well beaten curd. Cook till masala turns reddish again.

7. Reduce heat. Add red chilli powder, garam masala, haldi, amchoor and salt. Cook for 1 minute. Add ¼ cup water to get a thick, dry masala. Boil. Cook for 1 minute on low flame. Remove from fire.

8. Insert a little masala in between the florets of the fried cauliflower, especially from the backside.

9. To serve, arrange cauliflowers on a platter. Add ¼ cup water to masala to make it a masala gravy. Boil. Add ½ tsp salt or to taste. Pour over arranged cauliflowers. Heat in a microwave or oven. Alternately, heat the cauliflower in a kadhai in 1 tbsp oil at the time of serving. Heat the masala gravy separately. Arrange the hot cauliflowers on a serving platter. Pour hot gravy over it.

10. Sprinkle some boiled peas on it and on the sides. Serve.

Gobhi Bhare Tamatar

Tomatoes stuffed with a nutty cauliflower filling and the filling is sealed with a gramflour coating.

Serves 6-8

5 large firm tomatoes - cut into two halves

FILLING
½ of a medium cauliflower - grated
1 small boiled potato - mashed coarsely
½ tsp jeera
¼" piece ginger - finely grated
¾ tsp salt, ¼ tsp red chilli powder
½ tsp garam masala, ¼ tsp amchoor
2 tbsp kaju (cashewnuts) - chopped
1 tbsp kishmish (raisins)
¼ tsp sugar

TOPPING
3 tbsp besan (gram flour), a pinch of orange colour, a pinch of salt and ajwain

1. Heat 3 tbsp oil in a kadhai. Add jeera. When jeera turns golden, add ginger. Reduce heat. Saute for ½ minute. Add salt, red chilli powder, garam masala and amchoor.
2. Add cashew nuts and raisins. Stir for a few seconds.
3. Add potatoes. Cook for a minute.
4. Add grated cauliflower. Mix well. Add sugar. Cook covered for about 10 minutes, stirring frequently, till the cauliflower gets cooked.
5. Cut firm tomatoes into half. Scoop out the pulp. Rub a little salt inside and keep them upside down for 15 minutes.
6. Fill with cauliflower filling. Press well. Heat 2 tsp oil on a tawa.
7. Take out besan in a plate. Add a pinch of orange colour, salt and ajwain.
8. Holding the filling side up, invert the tomato in the besan to coat the top of the filling.
9. Invert the tomato in hot oil on the tawa with the filling side down.
10. Turn after a minute to slightly cook the other side too. Keep on fire for a short while, or the tomatoes turn limp. Turn when the side is done. Serve hot as a side dish.

Cheesy Peppers

Cheesy tomato rice stuffed in capsicums.

Picture on page 19   *Serves 10*

8 green, red or yellow peppers (simla mirch)
1 tsp salt
juice of 1 lemon
2 tsp ginger paste
2 tbsp oil

STUFFING
2 tbsp butter
1 cup uncooked rice - soaked for 1 hour
2 tbsp readymade tomato puree
1 onion - chopped finely
8-10 french beans - threaded and cut into small cubes
1 small carrot - cut into small cubes
100 gm mozzarella cheese - grated (1 cup)
1½ tsp salt, or to taste, ½ tsp pepper

TOPPING
4-5 tbsp grated cheese
2 tsp tomato ketchup to dot, a few coriander or mint leaves

1. Cut a thin slice from the top of the peppers. Pull out the stalk end and make it hollow. Cut the top in a zig-zag fashion (VVVV) with a sharp kitchen knife to make the peppers look decorative. Rub a little salt , lemon juice and ginger paste on the inner surface. Keep them upside down. Pour some oil on the outer surface. Rub the oil on the outer and inner surface and keep aside for 10 minutes.
2. For stuffing, heat butter in a heavy bottomed pan and fry the onions till transparent.
3. Add beans and carrots and stir fry for 2-3 minutes.
4. Drain the rice. Add rice and tomato puree. Stir fry gently for 2 minutes.
5. Add 2 cups water. Add salt and pepper. Boil. Cook covered on low flame for 10-12 minutes, till the rice is cooked. Remove from fire.
6. Sprinkle cheese all over on the rice. Do not stir. Cover and keep aside. The cheese melts and goes into the rice. Cool the rice mixture to stuff the peppers. Fill the peppers with this mixture. *Contd...*

7. Press well and keep aside till serving time. At the time of serving, heat a non stick pan or a flat bottomed kadhai. Put 2 tbsp oil and spread the oil to coat the pan.
8. Arrange filled peppers and cook covered on low heat for 5-7 minutes, changing the sides once or twice in-between, till the peppers get cooked and turn blackish at some places. Do not cook for a longer time as they will turn limp on doing so. Remove from pan. Sprinkle some cheese on top. Dot with tomato sauce and a sprig of parsley or mint. Serve.

Note: You may also microwave or cook peppers in a moderately hot oven at 180°C for 10 minutes. A few tomatoes can also be stuffed the same way to add colour to the pepper platter. Cook them only for 4 minutes or they turn limp.

Cheesy Peppers: Recipe on page 16 ➤

Ajwani Aloo Mirch

A quick dry vegetable, strongly flavoured with carom seeds.

Serves 4

2 large potatoes - cut into thin long fingers
3 capsicums - cut into thin long fingers
2 tbsp oil
1 tsp ajwain (carom seeds)
5-6 flakes garlic crushed or 1 tsp finely chopped ginger
3 tomatoes (250 gm) - grind to a puree
¼ tsp haldi
2 tsp dhania powder
1 tsp salt
½ tsp red chilli powder
½ tsp garam masala
1 tbsp tomato ketchup

1. Cut potatoes into ¼" thick slices. Cut each slice into thin fingers like potato chips. Soak in cold water to which 1 tsp salt has been added. Soak for 10 minutes. Drain and wipe dry. Deep fry all together on medium flame till golden brown and cooked. Keep aside.
2. Heat 2 tbsp oil. Add ajwain. Wait for a minute.
3. Add garlic or ginger. Let it change colour.
4. Add fresh tomato puree. Stir for 5-6 minutes till dry.
5. Add all masalas - haldi, dhania, salt, red chilli and garam masala. Stir till oil separates.
6. Add tomato ketchup. Add 2 tbsp water. Mix.
7. Add capsicums. Stir for 2 minutes. Keep aside.
8. At serving time add the fried potatoes. Stir to mix well. Serve hot as a side dish.

Note: Make the potato chips well browned and crisp.

Makhani Mirch Makai

Green chillies and baby corns in a simple yet delicious gravy.

Serves 5-6

10-12 pieces (150 gm) baby corns - cut lengthwise into 2 long pieces
6 big green chillies - slit & deseeded
1 large onion - ground to a paste
2 tbsp kaju (cashews) - soaked in warm water and ground to a paste
4 tomatoes - ground to a puree
1" piece ginger - grated
¼ tsp haldi, 1 tsp dhania powder (ground coriander), ½ tsp garam masala
1¼ tsp salt, or to taste, ½ tsp pepper, or to taste
1 cup milk, see note
½ cup cream (optional)

1. Heat 4 tbsp oil. Add green chillies and fry for 3-4 minutes till they turn slightly whitish. Remove from oil and keep aside.
2. Add baby corns and fry for 3-4 minutes till brown specs appear. Remove from oil and keep aside.

3. Heat the remaining oil. Add onion, fry till light brown.
4. Add haldi, dhania powder and garam masala. Stir for a minute.
5. Add fresh tomato puree. Cook for 5 minutes on low heat till dry and oil separates.
6. Add cashew paste. Mix.
7. Add 1 cup of water and boil. Add salt and pepper to taste. Add fried baby corns. Simmer on low flame for 10 minutes till thick.
8. Add grated ginger. Remove from fire and keep aside till serving time.
9. At serving time, add milk to the thick masala to get a gravy. Mix well. Keep on low heat, stirring continuously till it comes to a boil.
10. Add fried chillies & cream. Remove from heat & serve immediately.

Note:
- The milk should never be added to the hot tomato gravy. Let it cool down before adding the milk. Never boil the gravy too much after the milk has been added. It might curdle if done so.

- Choose green chillies which are thick, big and light green, as the small, dark green ones are hotter. Remember, to deseed them. After deseeding them, tap them gently to remove all the seeds.

Babycorn Jalfrezi

Serves 4

3+2 tbsp oil (5 tbsp)
½ tsp jeera (cumin seeds)
1¼ tsp mixed seeds (½ tsp sarson, ½ tsp kalonji, ¼ tsp methi daana)
15-20 curry leaves
2 onions - cut into half rings
¼ tsp haldi

MIX TOGETHER

¾ readymade cup tomato puree, 2 tsp tomato ketchup
2 tsp ginger-garlic paste or 2 tsp ginger-garlic - finely chopped
½ tsp red chilli powder, ½ tsp amchoor powder, 1 tsp dhania powder, 1 tsp salt

VEGETABLES

200 gms babycorns
1 carrot - cut diagonally into slices, ½ cup shelled peas (matar) - boiled
1 green capsicum - deseed and cut into thin fingers
1 long, firm tomato - cut into 4 and then cut into thin long pieces

1. Boil 4 cups water with 1 tsp salt and ½ tsp sugar. Add carrots after the water boils. Boil for 2 minutes till crisp-tender. Refresh in cold water.
2. Cut baby corns into half lenghtwise. Stir fry them in 3 tbsp oil in a flat kadhai for 4-5 minutes till golden brown. Keep them spaced out while frying. Remove from kadhai. Keep aside.

Step 2

3. Mix together - tomato puree, tomato ketchup, ginger, garlic, red chilli powder, dhania powder, amchoor and salt in a bowl. Keep aside.
4. Heat 2 tbsp oil in a kadhai. Add jeera and the mixed seeds. When jeera turns golden, reduce heat & add curry leaves and stir for a few seconds.
5. Add onions cook till golden. Add haldi. Mix.
6. Add the tomato puree mixed with dry masalas and stir on medium heat for 2 minutes.
7. Add the babycorns, carrot, peas, capsicums and tomatoes. Stir till well blended. Remove from fire. Serve hot.

Kadhai Makai

Corns in the usual kadhai masala, flavoured with fenugreek and coriander. The addition of some cream at the end makes all the difference.

Serves 4

200 gm baby corns (20 pieces approx.)
juice of ½ lemon
2 capsicums - cut into fingers
1-2 dry red chillies
1½ tsp saboot dhania (coriander seeds)
a pinch of methi daana (fenugreek seeds)
2 tsp ginger- garlic paste
2 onions - chopped
4 tomatoes - pureed in a grinder
1 tbsp kasoori methi (dry fenugreek leaves)
¼ tsp haldi, ½ tsp garam masala
½ tsp amchoor, 1¼ tsp salt, or to taste
½" piece ginger - cut into match sticks or shredded on the grater (1 tsp)
5 tbsp oil
¼ cup cream (optional)

1. Boil 4 cups water with 2 tsp salt and lemon juice. Add baby corns and boil for 2 minutes. Drain. Refresh in cold water. Cut into 2 pieces lengthwise if thick.
2. Warm red chillies and dhania saboot on a tawa, till slightly crisp and dry, for about 30 seconds.
3. Roughly grind red chillies and saboot dhania to a rough powder.
4. Heat 2 tbsp oil in a kadhai and add the boiled baby corns. Bhuno for 4-5 minutes till they start turning brown. Keep them spaced out while bhunoing and let them not overlap each other. Add the capsicum strips and stir fry for 2 minutes. Remove from kadhai and keep aside.
5. Heat 3 tbsp oil in a kadhai. Reduce flame. Add a pinch of methi daana, dhania-red chilli powder. Stir for 30 seconds. Add garlic or ginger paste.
6. Add onion. Cook till onions turn light golden.
7. Add tomatoes and stir for about 4-5 minutes on low heat till dry.
8. Add salt, kasoori methi, haldi, garam masala and amchoor. Mix well till oil separates. Add ½ cup water. Let it boil.
9. Add baby corns and capsicum. Cook for 2-3 minutes.
10. Reduce heat. Mix in the shredded ginger and cream. Remove from fire. Serve hot.

Haryaali Malai Kofta

Serves 6-8

KOFTAS (12-13)

100 gm paneer - mashed
2 slices bread - remove sides
3 tbsp curd
1/8 tsp baking powder
1 green chilli - chopped finely
1 tbsp finely chopped coriander
½ tsp salt & ½ tsp pepper, to taste
¼ tsp red chill powder
1½ tbsp maida (plain flour)
a few pieces of cashewnuts

GRAVY

4 tbsp oil
1 tsp dhania powder, ½ tsp red chilli powder
¼ tsp amchoor, ¼ tsp garam masala, salt to taste

Phool Dilkhush: Recipe on page 12 ➤

BOIL TOGETHER
½ kg spinach leaves - chopped, 1 green chilli - chopped
1" piece ginger - chopped

GRIND TOGETHER FOR GRAVY
2 onions, 2 tomatoes, 2 laung (cloves)

TADKA/TEMPERING
1 tbsp desi ghee
1" piece ginger - cut into match sticks
1 green chilli - slit lengthways
½ tsp red chilli powder

1. To prepare koftas, spread ¾ tbsp curd on each slice of bread to wet it. After spreading curd on both sides of bread, keep aside for a minute.
2. Mash the paneer well. Add baking powder, green chillies and coriander.
3. Mash the bread slices well and mix with the paneer. Add salt, pepper and red chilli powder to taste.
4. Add maida in the end. Mix well.
5. Make balls and stuff a piece of cashew in the centre.

6. Deep fry 4-5 pieces at a time, in medium hot oil and keep aside.
7. To prepare the gravy, wash palak leaves and chop roughly. Put leaves with a green chilli and ginger in a pan and cook covered on low heat for 3-4 minutes after it boils. Remove from fire. Cool.
8. After the spinach cools, grind to a paste and keep aside.
9. Grind onions, tomatoes and 2 laung to a paste.
10. Heat 4 tbsp oil. Add the onion - tomato paste and cook stirring till dry.
11. Add garam masala, dhania powder, red chilli powder, amchoor & salt to taste. Bhuno further for 1-2 minutes on low flame, till oil separates.
12. Add the ground spinach and bhuno for 2-3 minutes. Add ½ cup water to make a thin green gravy and bhuno for 5-7 minutes.
13. At serving time heat the spinach gravy and add the kofta. Stir gently on low flame for 1-2 minutes till the koftas are heated through. Remove from fire and transfer to a serving dish.
14. For the tadka, heat 1 tbsp desi ghee and add the ginger. When it turns brownish, shut off the flame. Add green chillies. Add red chilli powder and immediately pour the oil on the koftas in the serving dish. Mix lightly. Serve.

Achaari Palak Makai

Spinach combined with corn kernels and tempered with pickle spices.

Serves 4

1 cup boiled or tinned corn kernels (makai ke daane)
1 bundle spinach (700 gm) - chopped finely without the stems
1 tbsp kasoori methi (dry fenugreek leaves)
½ tsp sugar, ½ cup water
½ cup chopped coriander, 2 green chillies, 1" piece ginger - chopped
2 onions - ground to a paste
3 tomatoes - ground to a puree
¼ tsp haldi, 1 tsp salt, 2 tsp dhania powder, ½ tsp garam masala
1 cup milk

ACHAARI TADKA

½ tsp saunf, ½ tsp jeera (cumin seeds), ½ tsp rai or sarson
¼ tsp kalonji (nigella seeds), a pinch of methi daana
2 dry, red chillies
¼ tsp red chilli powder, preferably degi mirch

1. Mix chopped spinach with dry kasoori methi and sugar in a deep pan. Add ½ cup water and bring to a boil. Cook uncovered till soft, for about 4- 5 minutes on low heat, stirring in-between. Remove from fire. Cool. Grind the spinach along with the liquid, ½ cup coriander, green chillies and ginger to a puree. Keep aside.
2. Heat 3 tbsp oil. Add onion paste and stir till golden brown. Add tomatoes and cook till dry. Add haldi, salt, dhania powder and garam masala. Stir till oil separates.
3. Add corn and stir for 2 minutes. Add spinach paste and cook for 10 minutes.
4. Add milk and stir on low heat for 2 minutes. Remove to a serving dish.
5. For the tadka, heat 2 tbsp oil or ghee. Reduce heat. Collect together saunf, jeera, rai or sarson, kalonji and methi daana. Add all these together to the oil. When methi daana turns brown, add the dry red chillies and chilli powder. Remove from fire and pour over the spinach in the dish.

Kurkuri Ajwaini Bhindi

Amazingly crisp and crunchy with a strong flavour of carom seeds.

Serves 2-3

250 gm bhindi (lady fingers)
1 tsp ajwain (carom seeds)
¼ tsp haldi
2 tsp chaat masala
1 tsp chilli powder
1 tsp ginger or garlic paste
4-5 tbsp besan (gram flour)
½ tsp salt, or to taste
juice of ½ lemon (1 tbsp)
oil for frying

BHINDI

1. Wash and pat dry bhindi. Cut the head. Cut the bhindi into four lengthwise to get 4 long pieces from each bhindi. Place in a shallow bowl or paraat.
2. Heat oil in a kadhai for frying.
3. Sprinkle ajwain, haldi, chaat masala, ginger or garlic paste, dry besan and salt on the bhindi.
4. Sprinkle lemon juice and mix well to coat the bhindi with the spices.
5. Add half of the bhindi to hot oil and fry in 2 batches till crisp. Drain on absorbent paper.

Tip: Mix all the ingredients to the bhindi at the time of frying as the salt added releases moisture which can make the bhindi soggy.

Achaari Bhindi

An unusual combination of bhindi in a masala flavoured with pickle spices.
Do give it a try.

Picture on page 1   *Serves 4*

½ kg bhindi
4 big (300 gms) tomatoes - chopped finely
2 tsp ginger or garlic paste
15-20 curry leaves
½ tsp haldi
½ tsp red chilli powder, 1 tsp dhania powder
¾ tsp salt, or to taste

ACHARI SPICES
a pinch of hing (asafoetida)
1 tsp saunf (fennel)
½ tsp kalonji (onion seeds)
¼ tsp methi daana (fenugreek seeds)
½ tsp rai (mustard seeds)

1. Wash bhindi and wipe dry. Cut the tip of the head of each bhindi, leaving the pointed end as it is. Now cut the bhindi vertically from the middle making 2 smaller pieces from each bhindi. Heat oil in a kadhai and deep fry the bhindi on medium heat in 2 batches. Do not over fry the bhindi, it should retain it's green colour. Drain on a paper napkin. Keep aside.
2. Heat 2 tbsp oil and add ginger or garlic paste. Add curry patta and stir fry for a minute.
3. Add achari spices. Stir till methi daana turns brown.
4. Add haldi, chilli powder, dhania powder & salt. Stir for 30 seconds.
5. Add chopped tomatoes and stir for about 7-8 minutes or till oil separates.
6. Add fried bhindi. Sprinkle ¼ tsp salt and stir gently on slow fire for a few minutes till well mixed. Serve hot.

Matar Dhania Wale

Peas with a green coriander paste.

Serves 4-5

2 cups shelled peas
2 tbsp oil, a pinch of hing, ½ tsp jeera (cumin seeds)
¼ tsp kalonji, ½ tsp salt, or to taste
1 firm tomato - cut into 8 pieces and pulp removed

DHANIA CHUTNEY

2 cups chopped coriander leaves
4 flakes garlic, 1½" piece of ginger, 2 green chillies, juice of 1 lemon
1 tomato, ½ tsp salt, or to taste

1. Grind together all the ingredients of the dhania chutney.
2. Heat 2 tbsp oil in the pressure cooker. Add hing, jeera and kalonji.
3. When jeera turns brown, add peas. Bhuno for 2-3 minutes.
4. Add dhania chutney to peas and mix well. Add salt. Pressure cook to give 1 whistle. Open the cooker after pressure drops. Serve hot.

Kathal Laajawaab: Recipe on page 96 ➢

Kastoori Gajar Matar

Dry fenugreek is mixed with carrots and some green peas to make a very colourful dish. Milk is added to dry fenugreek leaves to freshen them.

Picture on page 1 *Serves 4*

3 carrots - peeled, cut into half lengthwise & sliced diagonally or
cut into ¼" cubes
1 packet (2 cups) kasoori methi (dried fenugreek leaves) - cleaned & soaked in
water for ½ hour
1½ cups shelled peas (matar) - boiled
1 large onion - chopped
4-5 kaju (cashewnuts)
1 cup milk
2 tbsp mustard oil or any refined oil
a pinch of sugar
1 tsp salt
½ tsp red chilli powder
½ tsp garam masala
a pinch of amchoor (dried mango powder)

1. Soak cleaned methi in water for at least ½ hour or even more. Strain.
2. Squeeze very well. Chop finely and keep aside.
3. Heat 1 tbsp oil in a heavy bottomed kadhai. Add kaju fry for a minute and remove from oil.
4. Heat 2 tbsp oil in the same kadhai. Add onion and cook till soft.
5. Add kasoori methi and milk.
6. Add carrots. Cook on low heat till carrots are done and the milk is almost dry.
7. Add a pinch of sugar. Mix well.
8. Add salt and red chilli powder. Cook for 1 minute.
9. Add peas. Add garam masala and amchoor. Uncover and stir fry for 2-3 minutes.
10. At serving time, sprinkle fried kaju and mix well. Serve hot.

Step 1

Step 2

Karaari Bharwaan Arbi

Serves 8

½ kg arbi (colocasia) of medium size

STUFFING

½ tsp ajwain (carom seeds), ½ tsp kalaunji (onion seeds)
¾ tsp red chilli powder, ¾ tsp garam masala
2 tsp dhania (coriander) powder, 1 tsp amchoor, 1 tsp salt, 1 tsp oil

COATING

3 tbsp suji (semolina)
3 tbsp besan (gram flour)
¼ tsp each of salt, garam masala and red chilli powder

MASALA

2 onions - cut into fine rings, 2 capsicums - cut into fine rings
2 tbsp oil, ½ tsp ajwain (carom seeds), a pinch of haldi
½ tsp salt, ¼ tsp red chilli powder, 1 tsp lemon juice
1 tomato - cut into thin long pieces without pulp
½ tsp tandoori masala or chaat masala

1. Boil 4 cups water with 2 tsp salt. Add arbi to boiling water. After the boil comes again, cover and cook for about 12 minutes till arbi is done.
2. Drain. Cool the arbi and peel it.
3. Make a lengthways slit in each arbi.
4. Mix all ingredients of stuffing, including oil. The oil binds the stuffing.
5. Fill about ¼ tsp of stuffing in each slit with a spoon. Press the arbi to flatten it slightly and also to close the slit.
6. Repeat with all the pieces.
7. Heat oil in a kadhai for frying. Mix the coating ingredients in a flat plate.
8. Sprinkle some water on the stuffed arbi pieces. Roll each piece of arbi in the dry suji-besan mix and deep fry 5-6 pieces at one time on medium heat till golden.
9. For the masala- heat 2 tbsp oil in a pan, add ajwain, wait for a minute.
10. Add onions and fry till light golden, add a pinch of haldi.
11. Add salt, red chilli powder and lime juice. Mix. Add capsicum rings and cook for a minute.
12. Add fried arbi, stir fry for 2 minutes. Add tomatoes, mix and remove from fire. Sprinkle chaat masala. Toss for a minute. Serve hot.

Arbi Ajwaini

Arbi combined with a masala of onion rings flavoured with carom seeds.

Serves 4

½ kg arbi (colocasia)
2 onions - cut into rings
½" piece ginger - chopped finely
2-3 green chillies - cut into thin long pieces
¼ tsp haldi
2 tomatoes - chopped
1 tsp ajwain (carom seeds)
½ tsp jeera (cumin seeds)
1 tsp dhania (coriander) powder
½ tsp salt, or to taste
½ tsp red chilli powder
½ tsp amchoor (dried mango powder)
½ cup chopped coriander

1. Pressure cook arbi with 3 cups water and 2 tsp salt to give one whistle. Keep on low flame for 4 minutes. Do not over boil. Peel and flatten each piece between the palms.
2. Heat 2 cups oil in a kadhai for frying. Put 4-5 pieces of flattened arbi at one time in oil. Fry till golden brown. Remove from oil. Keep aside.
3. Heat 2 tbsp oil in a clean kadhai. Reduce flame. Add ajwain and jeera. Cook till jeera turns golden.
4. Add onion rings and cook till soft. Add haldi and mix.
5. Add tomatoes and cook for 2 minutes till soft. Add ginger and stir for a minute.
6. Add chilli powder, amchoor, salt and dhania powder. Stir to mix well. Add 2-3 tbsp water. Boil.
7. Add fried arbi. Mix well.
8. Add hara dhania and green chillies. Stir fry for 2 minutes.

Note: If the arbi is not boiled in salted water, add a little extra salt.

Kofte Gajar Ke

Serves 6-8

KOFTAS (16 BALLS)

250 gm (4) carrots - peeled & grated finely
2 boiled potatoes - grated, 2 green chillies - deseeded & chopped finely
2 tbsp cornflour, a pinch of baking powder
1 tsp salt, or to taste, ½ tsp red chilli powder
½ tsp amchoor, ½ tsp garam masala
16 dry aloo bukhaaras (plums) - soaked for 20 minutes & deseeded or 16 kishmish

GRAVY

2 laung (cloves), 1" stick dalchini (cinnamon) - broken into 2-3 pieces
1 tbsp kasoori methi (dry fenugreek leaves)
½ tsp haldi, ½ tsp red chilli powder, ½ tsp garam masala
2 tsp dhania (coriander) powder, 1½ tsp salt or to taste, 2 tbsp coriander leaves
1 cup milk, see note

PASTE

3 onions, 3 red tomatoes, 2 green chillies, 8-10 flakes garlic, 1" piece ginger

1. Grate carrots finely. Squeeze them. Mix all ingredients given under the koftas in a shallow bowl. Knead the mixture well for 4-5 minutes till well blended. Form into 1" long oval balls or round balls. Insert a deseeded, soaked dry aloo-bhukhaara or a kishmish. Shape into a ball again.
2. Heat oil, for frying balls. Add only 2-3 balls at a time & carefully fry them on medium flame till they turn golden & get cooked from inside.
3. For gravy, grind all the ingredients given under paste to a smooth paste.
4. Heat 3 tbsp oil in a kadhai & fry dalchini and laung for a few seconds.
5. Add the onion and tomato paste. Cook till dry.
6. Add kasoori methi and all dry masalas. Stir fry for 5 minutes till oil separates.
7. Add 2½ cups water to get a thin gravy. Boil. Add salt & coriander leaves. Simmer on low flame for 5-6 minutes. Keep aside.
8. At serving time, mix 1 cup milk to the gravy and now keep on low heat. Add koftas. Bring to a boil, stirring, on low heat. Serve hot.

Note: The milk should never be added to the hot tomato gravy. Let it cool down before adding the milk. Never boil the gravy too much after the milk has been added. It might curdle if done so.

Gajar Methi

Try carrots with methi instead of the usual potatoes. The addition of garlic is optional.

Serves 4

2-3 carrots - peeled and cut into cubes
2 bunches (700 gm) fresh methi (fenugreek leaves)
4 tbsp mustard oil or any refined oil
3-4 flakes garlic - crushed
¼ tsp hing (asafoetida)
¾ tsp jeera (cumin)
1 tsp garam masala
½ tsp amchoor
1 tsp dhania powder
½ tsp red chilli powder
1½ tsp salt or to taste

1. Remove the hard stems of methi and chop very finely. Rub 1 tsp of salt and keep aside for 15-20 minutes.
2. Peel and cut carrots into tiny cubes.
3. Wash methi in several changes of water till clean. Squeeze methi well to drain out water and keep aside.
4. Heat mustard oil to smoking point. Remove from fire. After a few seconds, add garlic and hing.
5. Return to fire. Reduce flame. Add jeera. Let it turn golden.
6. Add methi leaves. Stir fry till the water evaporates. Cook further for 5 minutes.
7. Add carrots and stir fry for a minute.
8. Add salt, dhania powder, red chilli powder, garam masala and amchoor. Cook covered for about 8-10 minutes till carrots turn soft. Serve hot.

Makki Matar Khumb

Mushrooms with corn and peas in a delicious fenugreek flavoured white gravy.

Serves 4-5

200 gms mushrooms - preferably small in size
¾ cup corn niblets (daane of 1 large bhutta or tinned corn kernels)
1 cup shelled, boiled or frozen peas
4 tbsp kasoori methi (dry fenugreek leaves)
1 tsp ginger-garlic paste, a pinch of pepper
1 tbsp butter, 3 tbsp oil
2 onions - ground to a paste
½ cup thin fresh cream or malai
1 tsp salt, or to taste, ½ tsp red chilli powder, ½ tsp garam masala
a pinch of amchoor, 1 cup milk (approx.)

GRIND TOGETHER
½ stick dalchini (cinnamon), seeds of 2-3 chhoti illaichi (green cardamom)
3-4 laung (cloves), 4-5 saboot kali mirch (peppercorns)
2 tbsp cashewnuts (kaju)

1. Boil whole fresh corn or frozen corn kernels in 4 cups water with ¼ tsp haldi, 2 tsp sugar and 1 tsp salt to get soft, yellow, sweetish corn. If using tinned corn, simply drain the water and use.
2. Trim the stem of each mushroom. Leave them whole if small or cut them into 2 pieces, if big.
3. Heat 1 tbsp butter in a kadhai and add the mushrooms. Stir fry on high flame till dry and golden.
4. Add ginger-garlic paste, ½ tsp salt and a pinch of pepper. Stir for 1 more minute and remove from fire. Keep cooked mushrooms aside.
5. Grind together dalchini, seeds of chhoti illaichi, laung, kali mirch and cashews to a powder in a small mixer grinder.
6. Heat 3 tbsp oil. Add onion paste and cook on low heat till oil separates. Do not let the onions turn brown.
7. Add freshly ground masala-cashew powder. Cook for a few seconds.
8. Add kasoori methi & cream or malai, cook on low heat for 2-3 minutes till malai dries up. Add salt, chilli powder, garam masala & amchoor.
9. Add corn, peas, mushrooms & milk for thick gravy. Stir for a minute.
10. Add ½ cup water if the gravy appears too thick. Boil for 2-3 minutes.

Bharwaan Khumb Curry

Anaar & cheese stuffed in mushrooms & put in an illachi flavoured yellow gravy!

Serves 6-8

300 gm mushrooms (15-18 good size pieces)
juice of ½ lemon, 2 tsp salt
1 cup red kandhari anaar ke daane (fresh pomegranate)

FILLING
50 gms mozzarella or pizza cheese - grated finely (½ cup)
3 tbsp anaar ke daane, ¼ tsp black pepper, 2-3 big pinches of salt

GRAVY
3 onions, 1½" piece ginger, 3 dry red chillies
4 tbsp oil, 4-5 chhoti illaichi (green cardamoms) - pounded to open slightly
½ tsp garam masala, ½ tsp red chilli powder, ½ tsp haldi
1 tsp dhania powder, 1½ tsp salt, or to taste, 1 cup milk
1 tbsp finely chopped coriander & 1 tbsp cream - to garnish

1. Wash mushrooms and pull out the stalks. Hollow the mushrooms a little more with the help of a small scooper. Keep stalks aside.

2. Boil for 4-5 cups water with 2 tsp salt and juice of ½ lemon. Add the mushrooms. Boil for 2 minutes. Drain and refresh with cold water. Strain. Wipe to dry well.

3. Mix all ingredients of the filling and stuff each mushroom with it. Place mushrooms in a hot oven at 200°C for 5-7 minutes or till cheese melts Remove from oven and keep aside.

4. To prepare the gravy, blend the anaar ke daane with 1½ cups water in a mixer blender. Strain to get juice.

5. Trim the left over mushroom stalks. Grind mushroom stalks with onions, ginger and dry red chillies to a fine paste.

6. Heat 4 tbsp oil in a heavy kadhai. Add illaichi. Wait for 30 seconds.

7. Add the onion-mushroom paste. Cook on low flame for about 7-8 minutes till onions turn light brown.

8. Add masalas - garam masala, red chilli powder, haldi, dhania & salt.

9. Add anaar ka ras. Boil, simmer for 5 minutes. Reduce heat. Add milk to the gravy. Simmer on low flame for 5 minutes. Keep aside.

10. To serve, boil gravy. Pour in a serving dish. Arrange mushrooms on it. Heat in a microwave or an oven. Serve immediately, sprinkled with cream and coriander.

Mushroom Chettinad

A brown mushroom curry with the fiery flavours of the South! You can also use paneer instead of mushrooms for paneer chettinad.

Serves 4

200 gm mushrooms - trim stalk and cut each into 2 pieces
5-6 saboot kali mirch (peppercorns) - crushed coarsely (½ tsp)

ROAST SPICES TOGETHER
½ cup freshly grated coconut - remove brown skin before grating
1 tsp saboot dhania (coriander seeds)
½ tsp jeera (cumin seeds)
1 tsp saunf (fennel)
3-4 whole dry red chillies
seeds of 3 chhoti illaichi (green cardamom)
2-3 laung (cloves)
1" stick dalchini (cinnamon)

SOAK TOGETHER
1 tbsp khus khus (poppy seeds)
2 tbsp kaju (cashewnuts)

MASALA
1 onion - chopped finely
3 tomatoes - chopped finely
1" piece ginger
8-10 flakes garlic
3 tbsp curry leaves
juice of ½ lemon
½ tsp haldi (turmeric powder)
½ tsp red chilli powder
1 tsp salt, or to taste

1. Wash mushrooms and trim the stalks. Cut into 2 pieces.
2. Soak khus khus and kaju in ½ cup warm water for 15 minutes.
3. Heat 1 tbsp oil on a tawa and roast all spices together on low heat till fragrant, for about 2-3 minutes. Remove from tawa. Cool.

Contd...

4. Grind roasted spices, to a very smooth paste with in a small spice grinder, along with ginger-garlic and the khus and cashews with water. Keep paste aside.
5. Heat 3 tbsp oil in a kadhai and stir fry onions till light golden.
6. Add curry leaves. Wait for a minute.
7. Add the above ground paste. Saute for 1 minute on low heat.
8. Add chopped tomatoes, haldi, salt and chilli powder. Cook for 5-7 minutes till the tomatoes get well blended and oil separates.
9. Add mushrooms and lemon juice. Stir fry for 5 minutes. Mix well.
10. Add 1¼ cups water and coriander. Give one boil. Simmer on low heat for 4-5 minutes, stirring occasionally till thick gravy is ready.
11. Sprinkle crushed peppercorns. Remove from fire. Serve hot.

Stuffed Cabbage Rolls: Recipe on page 79 ➤

Khumb Nadiyaan Kinare

Mushrooms with peas and tomato pieces in masala.

Serves 4

200 gm mushrooms - each cut into 4 pieces
2 cups green peas - boiled with little sugar and salt
1 large tomato - finely chopped
1 large onion - finely chopped
1 large tomato - cut into 1" pieces
1 tsp salt
¼ tsp haldi
½ tsp garam masala
1 tsp dhania powder
½ tsp red chilli powder
2 tsp finely chopped ginger
1 green chilli - chopped
3-4 tbsp cream

1. Cut one tomato into 1" pieces and remove pulp and keep aside to be added at the end. Chop the second tomato finely and mix with the pulp of the first tomato.
2. Heat 3 tbsp oil. Add onions and stir fry till soft.
3. Add chopped tomato and the pulp of the first tomato. Stir for 2 minutes.
4. Add mushrooms, stir fry for a minute.
5. Reduce heat. Add salt, haldi, garam masala, dhania powder and red chilli powder. Cook for 5-7 minutes on low heat.
6. Add boiled peas, ginger and green chillies. Keep aside till serving time.
7. At the time of serving, heat the vegetable. Add 3-4 tbsp cream and tomato pieces. Stir for 2 minutes. Serve hot.

Baingan Mirch Ka Saalan

Brinjals in a tamarind gravy.

Serves 4

6 small brinjals - cut into 4 pieces lengthwise and sprinkled with salt
4-5 achaari hari or laal mirch (large green or red chillies), optional
a lemon sized ball of imli (tamarind)
5 tbsp oil
½ tsp sarson (mustard seeds), ½ tsp kalonji (onion seeds)
3 onions - finely chopped
a few curry leaves
2 tbsp cashews - soaked in 4 tbsp milk and ground to a paste
2 tbsp fresh cream

PASTE
2 tbsp til (sesame seeds)
1 tsp desiccated coconut (coconut powder)
6 flakes garlic, 1½" piece of ginger
2 tsp dhania (coriander) powder, ¼ tsp haldi (turmeric) powder
1 tsp jeera (cumin seeds), 1 tsp salt, 1 tsp fresh lemon juice

1. Wash the tamarind and put in a bowl with 1½ cups hot water. Mash and leave it to soak for 10 minutes.
2. Grind all ingredients given under paste to a smooth paste with a little water. Keep aside.
3. Pat dry the brinjals sprinkled with salt on a clean kitchen towel.
4. Heat 5-6 tbsp oil in pan. Reduce heat and fry the green chillies for 1½ minutes. Remove the chillies from the oil and keep aside. In the same oil, add the brinjals. Fry turning sides on medium heat till they change colour and turn brownish. Check with a knife and remove from oil when they turn soft.
5. Heat 2 tbsp oil in a kadhai. Add kalonji and mustard seeds. Wait for ½ minute till they crackle, add onions and curry leaves. Fry till onions turn golden brown.
6. Add the freshly ground spices and fry for 2 minutes.
7. Add cashew paste and stir to mix well.
8. Add 2 cups water and stir. Pour strained tamarind juice. Boil. Simmer for 7-8 minutes on low heat.
9. Add the green chillies and brinjals. Cook for 5 minutes on low heat.
10. Add cream and remove from fire. Serve with rice or chappati.

Chutney Waale Bharwaan Baingan

A dry dish of brinjals which are stuffed with a nutty coriander paste.

Serves 6

400 gm (12) small round brinjals
a pinch of hing (asafoetida)
3 dry, whole red chillies
¼ tsp methi daana (fenugreek seeds)
1 onion - finely sliced
¼ tsp salt, ¼ tsp garam masala
¼ tsp haldi, ¼ tsp red chilli powder
juice of ½ lemon
4 tbsp oil

DRY ROAST TOGETHER ON A TAWA (GRIDDLE)
2 tsp til (sesame seeds)
2 tsp saboot dhania (coriander seeds)
½ tsp jeera (cumin seeds)
2 whole, dry red chillies

NUTTY CHUTNEY
½ cup fresh coriander leaves
3 tbsp roasted peanuts (moongphali), 1 tomato
¾ tsp salt, or to taste, ¼ tsp sugar, ¼ tsp amchoor
1" piece ginger, 5-6 flakes garlic, 2 green chillies

1. Wash and slit brinjals in four, leaving the stem intact. The brinjals should be intact at the base.
2. Mix the freshly roasted masalas with the ingredients of the nutty chutney and grind together to a thick paste.
3. Fill the brinjals with this paste.
4. Heat oil in pressure cooker. Add the hing, red chillies and methi daana.
5. When methi daana turns golden, add the sliced onion and fry till light golden.
6. Add salt, garam masala, haldi and red chilli powder.
7. Add the brinjals. Gently fry them on low flame for 3-4 minutes or till the skin changes colour.
8. Add ½ cup water. Scrape the masala sticking to the bottom of the cooker. Close the cooker and pressure cook to give 1 whistle. Keep on low heat for 3 minutes. Remove from fire. Sprinkle lemon juice. Serve.

Hyderabadi Baingan

Serves 4

250 gms small baingan (5-6 pieces), 6-7 tbsp oil

FILLING

2 tbsp til (sesame seeds)
a small piece of fresh coconut - remove brown skin and grate finely (3-4 tbsp)
½ tsp salt, ½ tsp red chilli powder, ½ tsp amchoor powder, ¼ tsp sugar

MASALA GRAVY

2 onions, 1" piece ginger, 2 dry whole red chillies, 3 tomatoes - grind all together
1 tsp dhania powder, ½ tsp amchoor (dried mango powder)
1 tsp salt or to taste, ½ tsp garam masala, 2 pinches sugar

1. Wash baingans. Make two cross cuts from the top, leaving the end part intact.
2. Mix all ingredients of the filling together. Fill 2 tsp filing in each baingan.
3. Heat 6-7 tbsp oil. Put the baingans in the oil and cook for 3- 4 minutes stirring occasionally. Cover and cook for another 15 minutes till soft.

Gently keep turning the baingans occasionally till very soft. Pick up the brinjals and keep aside. Drain the excess oil from the kadhai and keep aside.

4. To prepare the masala, grind onions, ginger, red chillies and tomatoes together to a paste.

5. Heat 4 tbsp oil in a kadhai. Add the onion - tomato paste. Cook till almost dry.

6. Add dhania powder, amchoor, garam masala and salt. Cook on low flame till oil separates.

7. Add 1½ cups hot water to get a gravy. Simmer gravy for 5-7 minutes on low flame. Keep gravy aside.

8. To serve, heat baingans separately. Sprinkle 2 pinches sugar, ¼ tsp amchoor and ¼ tsp salt on the baingans while being heated.

9. Heat the gravy separately.

10. Pour the gravy in a low sided dish. Carefully pick up each hot baingan and arrange neatly over the gravy.

11. Put a few drops of cream or well beaten curd on the gravy (not on the baingans) and arrange few boiled peas over the drops of cream. Serve.

Shahi Kaju Aloo

Potatoes coated with curd and cashew masala flavoured with black cumin.

Serves 6

4 potatoes
2 tbsp cashew halves
4 tbsp kaju (cashews) - soaked in ¼ cup water
1 tbsp chopped ginger
1 tsp chopped garlic
4 tbsp oil
1 tsp shah jeera (black cumin)
1 tej patta (bay leaf)
2 onions - chopped
¼ tsp haldi (turmeric), ½ tsp garam masala
1 tsp salt, or to taste
¼ cup yogurt - whisked to make it smooth
¼ cup milk mixed with ½ cup water
oil for frying

1. Wash potatoes and peel. Cut potatoes into 1" pieces.
2. Deep fry the potatoes on medium heat till well cooked and they turn to a deep golden brown. Check with a knife to see that they are done. Keep aside. Fry the cashew halves also to a nice golden colour in the same oil. Remove from oil and keep aside.
3. Grind soaked kaju, ginger and garlic to a paste in a small coffee or spice grinder. Keep cashew paste aside.
4. Heat 4 tbsp oil in a heavy bottomed kadhai. Add shah jeera and tej patta. Let jeera change colour.
5. Add onions and cook on low heat till onions turn soft but do not let them turn brown.
6. Add haldi, garam masala and salt. Stir to mix well.
7. Add cashew paste. Cook for 1 minute.
8. Add yogurt and stir fry till water evaporates. Cook till dry.
9. Add milk and about ½ cup water to get a gravy. Boil and simmer uncovered for just 2-3 minutes.
10. Add the fried potatoes to the gravy and simmer on low heat. Cook on low heat till the gravy gets thick and coats the potatoes.
11. Add the fried cashew halves. Mix well. Serve hot with rotis or paranthas.

Aloo Khaas

Slices of potatoes sandwiched with paneer filling and put in a semi-dry masala.

Picture on cover   *Serves 4*

2 large round potatoes - peeled, cut into paper thin round slices, lengthwise
3 tbsp maida, 4 tbsp water, ¼ tsp salt, ¼ tsp red chilli powder

FILLING

100 gms paneer - grated finely
8-10 kishmish - soaked in water and chopped, 5-6 cashewnuts (kaju) - chopped
¼ tsp salt, a pinch of red chilli powder, a pinch of pepper

MASALA

1½ onions - chopped finely
2 tomatoes, ¼" piece ginger, 2 flakes garlic, 1 dry red chilli
3 tbsp oil, 1 tej patta (bay leaf), 2 laung (cloves)
¼ tsp red chilli powder, ½ tsp dhania (coriander) powder
¼ tsp haldi, ¾ tsp salt or to taste, 1 tsp chilli-garlic tomato sauce

1. Peel potatoes. Cut into very thin round slices. Boil in salted water for 2 min.
2. Mix all the ingredients of the filling lightly with a spoon. Do not mash.
3. Sandwich 1 tsp of filling between 2 slices of potatoes. Press well.
4. Prepare a thin paste with maida, 6 tbsp water, salt and chilli powder.
5. For masala, grind ginger, garlic, tomatoes & chilli to a paste in a blender.
6. Heat oil. Add tej patta. Add onion and cook till golden.
7. Add tomato paste. Cook till it turns dry.
8. Add haldi, dhania and red chilli powder. Add laung. Cook on slow flame for 2-3 minutes till oil separates.
9. Add ¾ cup water. Boil. Add salt and chilli garlic tomato sauce. Simmer on low flame for 5-7 minutes. Keep aside.
10. At serving time, heat a sandwich toaster or an oven rack. Brush it well with oil. Dip first the sides of the sandwiched potato slices in the maida batter and then the whole piece in the batter. Place the pieces on the greased sandwich toaster or on the hot grill of the oven. Press the pieces on the toaster or the grill to get lines on the aloo. Cook till light brown lines appear on the aloo. Turn pieces and brown both sides.
11. To serve, heat masala and put in a shallow dish. Arrange the hot aloos on it. Sprinkle some masala on the aloos too. Serve hot.

Dum Aloo Chutney Wale

Whole potatoes simmered in a tangy mint flavoured gravy.

Serves 5-6

8 baby potatoes - keep whole or 3 potatoes - each cut into 4 pieces

CHUTNEY

1 cup chopped fresh coriander, ½ small raw mango or ½ tsp amchoor
½ cup poodina (mint)
½ tsp salt, ½ tsp sugar

GRAVY

2 onions - ground to a paste
2 tsp ginger paste, 2 tsp garlic paste
1 tsp jeera (cumin) seeds
1 tsp red chilli powder
1 cup yoghurt - beat till smooth and mix with 1½ cups water
2 tbsp cashewnuts (kaju) - ground to a paste with a little water
1 tomato - chopped finely
½ tsp garam masala, 1 tsp salt, or to taste

1. Peel and wash potatoes. Heat oil in a kadhai and deep fry over low heat until cooked and light brown in colour. Keep aside.
2. For the chutney, put all ingredients in a blender and make a paste. Keep chutney aside.
3. Beat yoghurt in a bowl. Add cashew paste and 1½ cups water. Mix well.
4. Heat 4 tbsp oil in a kadhai.
5. Add onion paste, stir over low heat until transparent. Do not brown the onions.
6. Add the ginger and garlic pastes and stir until the oil leaves the masala.
7. Add jeera, stir for a minute.
8. Add chutney and red chilli powder, stir for ½ minute.
9. Remove from fire. Then add yoghurt, cashews and water mix, stirring continuously on low heat till it comes to a boil.
10. Now add the fried potatoes and salt. Simmer uncovered for 5 minutes until the oil leaves the masala and the gravy turns thick.
11. Add tomatoes and garam masala, stir and bring to a boil. Serve.

Note: Do not cover the kadhai while cooking.

Broccoli Tandoori

Broccoli florets with long stalks are flavoured with carom seeds and barbecued.

Serves 4

2 small broccoli - cut into medium sized florets with long stalks
2 tsp salt
1 tsp sugar

1ST MARINADE

juice of 1 lemon (3-4 tsp)
¾ tsp carom seeds (ajwain)
1 tsp salt, ½ tsp red chilli powder

2ND MARINADE

1 cup thick yogurt - hang for 20 minutes in a muslin cloth
½ cup thick cream
2 tsp ginger paste
½ tsp ajwain
½ tsp red chilli paste, optional
¾ tsp salt, 1 tsp tandoori masala or chaat masala

1. Boil 5-6 cups of water in a large pan. Add 2 tsp salt and 1 tsp sugar to the water. Add broccoli pieces to the boiling water. Boil. Keep on boiling for 2 minutes. Drain. Refresh in cold water. Wipe broccoli well with a clean kitchen towel.
2. Spread the broccoli on a flat plate and sprinkle the ingredients of the 1st marinade. Mix well. Marinate the broccoli for 15 minutes.
3. Drain the broccoli of any excess liquid.
4. Mix all the ingredients of the 2nd marinade. Check salt and add more if needed. Add the broccoli to it and mix well. Insert the marinate in between the florets of the broccoli, especially from the backside. Keep in the refrigerator till the time of serving.
5. Brush the grill of the oven or gas tandoor with some oil. Place the broccoli spears on it and barbecue them in a gas oven for 10 minutes or grill in a preheated electric oven at 210°C/410°F for 5 minutes. Baste (pour on the broccoli) with some oil in between and grill further for 5 minutes. Do not over grill it, it turns too dry. Serve hot as a side dish.

Cheesy Broccoli Koftas

Picture on facing page   *Serves 4-6*

1 medium broccoli (hari gobhi) - grated along with tender stalks (2 cups grated)
1 potato - boiled and grated
2 tbsp roasted peanuts (moongphali) - crushed coarsely
½ tsp coarsely crushed saboot kali mirch (peppercorns)
½ tsp salt, ¼ tsp garam masala, ¼ tsp amchoor
1½ tbsp cornflour, a pinch of baking powder
1 cheese cube (20 gm) - cut into 10 pieces, ½ tbsp butter

GRAVY

2 onions and 1" piece ginger - ground to a paste together
2 tbsp cashewnuts (kaju) and 2 tbsp magaz (watermelon seeds) - soaked in
½ cup hot water for 5 minutes or use 4 tbsp of kaju (cashews)
4 tbsp dahi (yogurt), 3 tbsp oil
1 tsp kasoori methi (dry fenugreek leaves), 1 tsp garam masala
½ tsp red chilli powder, 1¼ tsp salt, or to taste
½ cup cream mixed with ½ cup milk

1. Grate the broccoli florets and the tender stems very finely.
2. Heat butter in a pan. Add grated broccoli. Add ¼ tsp salt. Stir on medium heat for 3-4 minutes on low heat. Remove from heat.
3. To broccoli, add grated potato, peanuts, salt, crushed peppercorns, garam masala, amchoor, cornflour and baking powder. Make balls.
4. Flatten a ball and put a small piece of cheese in it. Make a ball again.
5. Deep fry 2-3 balls at a time till golden. Drain on paper napkins.
6. For gravy, drain kaju & magaz, grind them along with curd to a paste.
7. Heat 3 tbsp oil. Add onion & ginger paste. Stir fry onion paste on low flame till oil separates & it turns transparent. Do not let it turn brown.
8. Gradually add curd-cashewnut mixture, stirring continuously. Bhuno for 4-5 minutes till masala turns thick and oil separates.
9. Add kasoori methi, garam masala, red chilli & salt. Stir for 1-2 minutes.
10. Reduce heat. Add cream mixed with milk. Stir to mix well.
11. Add 2 cups water. Boil. Simmer for 2-3 minutes, on low flame, stirring constantly. Remove from fire and keep aside till serving time.
12. At serving time, add enough water (½-1 cup) to get a thin gravy. Add koftas. Keep on low heat & stir continuously till it boils. Keep on low heat for 2-3 minutes till koftas turn soft. Serve hot.

Hari Gobhi Besani Tukri

Whole broccoli, batter fried and served in the tandoori style.

Serves 4

1 very small broccoli

MARINADE

2 tbsp lemon juice, 1 tsp salt
½ tsp red chilli powder, ½ tsp ajwain (carom seeds), 1 tbsp ginger paste

BATTER

½ cup besan (gram flour), ¼ cup milk, approx.
1 tsp ginger paste, ½ tsp ajwain
1 tbsp chopped coriander
½ tsp salt, ¼ tsp red chilli powder, ¼ tsp garam masala

SALAD

1 tomato - cut into four pieces, a few kheera slices and some onion rings

TO SPRINKLE

some chat masala

1. Remove most of the stem of broccoli leaving about 1", so that the florets stay together. Boil 8 cups water with 2 tsp salt and 1 tsp sugar. Put the whole broccoli in it. Put the broccoli with stem side down. See that the whole broccoli is dipped in water. Bring to a boil again. Boil for 2 minutes till the stalks turn soft. Check with a knife. Remove from fire. Remove from water and refresh in cold water. Wipe dry with a clean kitchen towel.
2. Mix all ingredients of the marinade. Insert the marinate in between the florets of the broccoli, especially from the backside. Keep aside for 15 minutes.
3. Mix all ingredients of the batter in a deep big bowl. Add enough milk to get a thick coating batter.
4. Heat oil for deep frying in a kadhai. Dip the broccoli in the batter. Spread the left over batter nicely with the hands on the broccoli to cover nicely.
5. Carefully put in hot oil and deep fry till light yellow on medium heat. Reduce heat and fry on low heat till golden brown. Remove from fire. Cut into four pieces with a sharp long knife on a chopping board.
6. Sprinkle some chaat masala on the broccoli tukris. Serve immediately along with salad sprinkled with some chaat masala.

Stuffed Cabbage Rolls

A very unusual baked dish. Whole cabbage leaves are filled with cottage cheese filling, placed on a bed of sweet and sour sauce and baked. This combination makes this dish really amazing! Must give it a try.

Serves 6-8   *Picture on page 57*

1 big cabbage - take 8 outer big leaves

FILLING

2 onions - chopped
1½ cups paneer - crumbled (200 gm)
1½ cups readymade tomato puree, 1 tsp vinegar
2 flakes garlic - crushed
4 tbsp oil
1 tsp sugar, ¼ tsp haldi, ¾ tsp salt, ½ tsp pepper

1. To break the outer leaves, cut leaves from the stalk end and gently pull from the cut end to get a whole leaf.
2. Boil 6-7 cups of water in a large pan with 2 tsp of salt and 1 tsp sugar.

Contd...

Add cabbage leaves to the boiling water. Cook cabbage in boiling salted water for atleast 3- 4 minutes till soft. Hard leaves do not taste good! Drain and cool.

3. Heat 2 tbsp oil. Add onion and cook till golden.
4. Add haldi and the paneer. Mix well. Add ½ tsp salt and ¼ tsp pepper to taste. Stir for 1 minute and remove from fire.
5. For sauce, heat 2 tbsp oil and fry the garlic till it just changes colour. Add the tomato puree, vinegar, sugar, ¾ tsp salt and ½ tsp pepper. Cook for 2 minutes. Remove from fire and check seasonings. Keep aside.
6. Spread a cabbage leaf on a flat surface. Cut off the hard end portion of the leaf.
7. Divide the paneer mixture into 8 portions. Place one portion of paneer in the centre of a cabbage leaf. Spread it along the width of the leaf and then roll. Pierce a toothpick on the hard central vein of the leaf.
8. Spread 3-4 tbsp sauce at the bottom of a greased baking dish.
9. Place the rolls close together in the baking dish.
10. Spread the left over sauce on the cabbage rolls.
11. Cover with aluminium foil and bake in a preheated oven at 180°C/ 350°F/Gas mark 4 for 20 minutes.

Cabbage Peanut Poriyal

A dry, spicy and crunchy South Indian side dish.

Serves 4

½ kg cabbage (1 medium) - chopped finely
½ cup peanuts (moongphali) - roasted
1½ tsp salt, or to taste

TEMPERING (CHOWNK)
4 tbsp oil
1 tsp rai (mustard seeds)
½ tsp jeera (cumin seeds)
2 tsp dhuli urad dal (split black gram)
2 tsp channa dal (bengal gram dal)
2 dry, red chilli - broken into bits
½ tsp hing (asafoetida)
¼ cup curry leaves

PASTE (GRIND TOGETHER)
2 green chillies
4- 5 tbsp grated coconut - remove the brown skin and then grate
1 onion - chopped
1 tsp jeera (cumin seeds)
2 tbsp curd

1. Heat oil. Reduce heat. Add all ingredients of tempering.
2. When dals turn golden, add the chopped cabbage. Mix well.
3. Add salt and 2 tbsp water. Mix well.
4. Add peanuts. Cover and cook on low heat for 7-8 minutes till cabbage turns tender.
5. Add the coconut paste. Stir fry for 3-4 minutes. Serve hot.

Note: You can make any poriyal in the same way - carrot, beetroot or capsicum.

Safed Jalpari

The water vegetable - lotus stem is coated with a white yogurt paste and stir fried to a delicious dry dish.

Serves 4   *Picture on page 85*

300 gm (2 medium) bhein or kamal kakri (lotus stem) - cut into diagonal thick pieces
3 onions - each cut into 4 pieces and separated
2 tbsp oil
1 tsp ajwain (carom seeds)
¼ tsp haldi, ¼ tsp salt, ¼ tsp red chilli powder
2-3 tbsp chopped coriander

MARINADE
1½ cups curd - hang for ½ hour
1 tsp ajwain (carom seeds)
1 tbsp finely chopped coriander, 1½ tbsp besan (gram flour)
1 tbsp ginger garlic paste, 1 tbsp oil
1 tsp salt

½ tsp red chilli powder, ½ tsp haldi, 1½ tsp dhania powder
½ tsp garam masala

TO SERVE
some chaat masala

1. Peel bhein. Cut into diagonal pieces of 1½" thickness.
2. Put bhein in a pan with 3- 4 cups water and 1 tsp salt. Keep on fire. Boil. Reduce heat and cook covered for about 10 minutes on low heat. Remove from fire. Drain water. Cut into 2 pieces lengthwise.
3. Mix all ingredients of the marinade together.
4. Add the boiled pieces of bhein to the marinade. Mix well to coat nicely.
5. Heat 2 tbsp oil in a kadhai. Add ajwain and wait till golden.
6. Add onions. Stir till golden.
7. Add haldi, salt and red chilli powder. Mix.
8. Add marinated bhein along with all the marinade. Cook on low heat, keeping the vegetable spread out. Cook till bhein turns golden.
9. Add the coriander and mix well. Serve sprinkled with chaat masala.

Safed Jalpari: Recipe on page 83 ➢

Peshawari Bhein

An unusual style to make crunchy lotus stem.

Serves 4

250 gm bhein or kamal kakri (lotus stem), choose thick ones
1" piece ginger
4-5 flakes garlic
2 green chillies
½ tsp ajwain (carom seeds)
1 tsp lemon juice
1 tbsp curd
¾ tsp salt
½ tsp red chilli powder
5-6 tbsp oil
2 tbsp atta (wheat flour)

1. Choose thick lotus stem (bhein). Cut bhein diagonally into ½" thick, slanting pieces. Wash well. Use a toothpick to clean if it is dirty. Boil in salted water till soft; or pressure cook in 1 cup water to give one whistle. Keep on low flame for 8-10 minutes.
2. Grind ginger, garlic, green chillies and ajwain to a paste.
3. Add lemon juice, curd, salt and red chilli powder to the above paste. Mix well.
4. Strain the boiled bhein. Dry them on a clean kitchen towel.
5. Apply the paste all over on the bhein. Keep aside for 1 hour.
6. At serving time, heat 5-6 tbsp oil. Reduce flame. Add atta. Cook for ½ -1 minute till the atta turns golden brown.
7. Add the marinated (rubbed with paste) bhein and stir fry for 5-6 minutes on low flame till the atta coats the bhein.
8. Sprinkle some amchoor powder and garam masala. Stir fry for 2-3 minutes till they turn dry and crisp. Serve.

Note: At the time of buying bhein, see that both the **ends** are **closed.** The closed ends prevent the dirt from going inside. Do not buy very thin bhein.

Punjabi Bhein Masala

Stuffed pieces of lotus stem, coated with flour.

Serves 4

300 gm (2 medium) bhein or kamal kakri (lotus stem), thick pieces
4 tbsp oil
2 tbsp atta (whole wheat flour)

FILLING (MIX TOGETHER)
2" piece ginger - crushed to a paste
8-10 flakes garlic - crushed to a paste
1 tsp salt
½ tsp red chilli powder, ½ tsp haldi
½ tsp amchoor
1½ tsp dhania powder
¾ tsp garam masala
1 tsp oil

1. Peel bhein. Wash well. Use a toothpick to clean if it is dirty. Cut into 1½" long pieces.
2. Put bhein in a pressure cooker with 1 cup water and ½ tsp salt. Boil in salted water till soft; or pressure cook in 1 cup water to give one whistle. Keep on low flame for 8-10 minutes. Remove from fire.
3. Strain the boiled bhein. Dry them on a clean kitchen towel. Keep aside.
4. Mix all ingredients of the filling together.
5. Make a slit in each boiled piece of bhein and fill the stuffing with the knife as you keep making the slit. Fill all the pieces and keep the left over filling aside.
6. Heat 4 tbsp oil in a large kadhai. Add 2 tbsp atta. Bhuno for 2 minutes on low heat.
7. Add the left over ginger-garlic filling and bhuno for a few seconds.
8. Add the bhein and stir fry for 5-7 minutes on medium flame till well browned. While bhunoing the bhein, spread out the vegetable in the kadhai so that all the pieces get well browned and turn crisp. Do not collect them in the centre of the kadhai.
9. Add fresh coriander and mix well. Serve hot with paranthas.

Other Vegetables

Bharwaan Parwal

Parwals stuffed with paneer and potato filling!

Serves 4

250 gm (8 medium parwal)

MARINATION
1 tbsp lemon juice
½ tsp red chilli powder, ½ tsp haldi, ½ tsp salt

FILLING
50 gm paneer - grated (½ cup)
1 small potato - boiled and cut into tiny cubes
½" piece ginger - chopped finely
1 tsp hara dhania (fresh coriander) - chopped
½ tsp amchoor (mango powder)
¼ tsp garam masala
¼ tsp kala namak, salt to taste
a few kaju (cashewnuts) - chopped, a few kishmish (raisins)

GRAVY
1 tbsp desi ghee/2 tbsp oil
½ tsp jeera (cumin seeds), a pinch hing (asafoetida)
¾ cup dahi - well beaten, 2½ tsp dhania (coriander) powder
½ tsp red chilli powder, salt to taste, ½ tsp haldi
1 tomato - pureed in a mixer, ½ tsp garam masala
1 tbsp roasted cashewnuts (kaju) - ground to a powder
¾ tsp salt or to taste

GARNISH
grated paneer, toasted almonds, ½ tomato - cut finely

1. Wash, peel, slit each parwal. Scoop out a little and remove seeds.
2. Mix all the ingredients of the marinade and rub the parwal - inside and out, with this marinade. Keep aside for 15 minutes.
3. Heat oil in kadhai and deep fry the marinated parwal over medium heat for 5-7 minutes or until cooked. Remove on absorbent paper to drain the excess oil.
4. Mix all the ingredients of the filling with the paneer and potato and divide them into 8 equal portions.

5. Stuff a portion of the filling in each parwal, pressing to ensure it is firmly packed. Keep aside.
6. To prepare the gravy, soak hing in 1 tbsp of water.
7. Beat dahi in a bowl and mix dhania powder, red chilli & haldi powder.
8. Heat ghee/oil in a handi or kadhai, add cumin seeds, stir over medium heat until they begin to pop. Add hing, stir for few seconds.
9. Remove handi from heat and stir in the dahi mixture, return handi to heat and bhuno until dry and the ghee leaves the sides.
10. Add the tomato puree, bhuno until the ghee/oil leaves the sides.
11. Add cashewnut powder and bhuno for a minute.
12. Add 1 cup of water, bring to a boil, reduce to low heat, simmer for 4-5 minutes, stirring occasionally, until the water is reduced slightly.
13. Add the stuffed parwal and simmer, stirring occasionally and carefully, for 5-6 minutes or until the gravy is of medium thick consistency.
14. Remove the parwal to a serving dish, pour on the gravy, garnish with grated paneer, toasted almonds and tiny tomato pieces. Serve with poori or phulka.

Saunfiyan Karela Subzi

Round slices of bitter gourd in a fennel flavoured masala.

Serves 4

350 gm (7 medium) karelas (bitter gourd) - peeled, cut into slices, rubbed with
2 tbsp vinegar and 1 tsp salt & kept away for ½ hour atleast

¾ tsp saunf (fennel)

3 onions - sliced

1 green chilli - deseeded and chopped

1" piece ginger - chopped

3 tomatoes - chopped

2 tsp dhania powder

½ tsp garam masala

¾ tsp salt

¾ tsp red chilli powder

oil to deep fry

1. Peel karelas. Cut them into round slices. Do not make the slices too thin as they turn too crisp on frying if very thin.

2. Sprinkle 2 tbsp vinegar and 1 tsp salt on them. Rub well. Keep aside for atleast ½ hour.
3. Wash well. Squeeze. Wash 2-3 times. Squeeze well to drain out all the bitterness alongwith water.
4. Heat oil in a kadhai for frying. Add the squeezed karelas and fry till golden brown. Drain and keep aside.
5. Heat 2 tbsp oil. Add saunf. When it changes colour, add the onions. Stir fry till light brown.
6. Add ginger and green chillies. Mix well.
7. Add tomatoes. Stir fry for 2-3 minutes till they turn soft.
8. Add dhania powder, garam masala, salt and red chilli powder. Stir for 2 minutes.
9. Add the fried karelas. Stir fry for 1-2 minutes.
10. Add more vinegar (1-2 tsp) to taste. Cook further for a few minutes. Serve hot with chappatis.

Note: Sirka (vinegar) removes the bitterness of the karelas and also adds taste to them.

Kathal Laajawaab

Boiled kathal (not the usual fried) coated lightly with masala.

Picture on page 39   *Serves 6*

500 gm kathal (jack fruit)
¾ tsp salt, or to taste
1 tsp dhania powder
½ tsp garam masala
¼ tsp haldi
1 tsp amchoor
½ tsp red chilli powder
5 tbsp oil
seeds of 1 moti illaichi (brown cardamom) - crushed
1 tbsp green coriander

GRIND TOGETHER TO A PASTE
1 onions - chopped roughly
2 large tomato - chopped roughly
1 green chilli, 1" piece ginger, 6-8 flakes garlic

1. Rub oil on your hands. Cut the whole big piece of kathal from the middle into two pieces. Remove skin. Cut widthwise from the centre of each piece. This way you get two big strips of kathal. Now further divide each strip into smaller pieces about 1" thickness, carefully to keep the shreds of the piece together . Then further divide into ½" thick pieces.
2. Boil 5 cups water with 2 tsp salt and ½ tsp haldi. Add kathal and boil uncovered for 7-8 minutes till a little soft. Keep it firm and crisp and do not over boil. Drain and keep aside.
3. Heat oil. Add onion-tomato paste and cook for 3-4 minutes. Add salt and all the masalas. Cook further for 5-7 minutes on low heat till oil separates.
4. Add the boiled kathal. Mix well gently and cook covered for 6-8 minutes on low heat till the vegetable blends well with the masala.
5. Sprinkle crushed illaichi. Mix. Serve hot garnished with chopped coriander.

Rajasthani Bharwaan Lauki

Picture on page 2   *Serves 4-6*

500 gm lauki (bottle gourd) - medium thickness

FILLING
200 gm paneer - crumbled (mash roughly)
1 tsp chopped ginger, 1 green chilli - chopped, 2 tbsp chopped green coriander
8-10 cashewnuts (kaju) - chopped, 8-10 kishmish (raisins) - soaked in water
¾ tsp salt or to taste

MASALA
2 tbsp oil or ghee, 2 laung (cloves), 2 tej patta (bay leaves)
2 chhoti illaichi (green cardamoms), 1" stick dalchini (cinnamon)

TOMATO PASTE (Grind Together)
3 tomatoes, 1 green chilli, ½" piece ginger
½ tsp red chilli powder, 1 tsp dhania powder, ¼ tsp haldi, ¾ tsp salt
½ tsp jeera (cumin seeds), ¼ tsp sugar

1. Peel lauki. Cut vertically into two pieces from the centre to get 2 smaller pieces.
2. Boil in salted water, covered, for about 10 minutes, till done. Remove from water and cool.
3. Scoop seeds from both the pieces of the lauki and make them hollow.
4. Mix paneer, ginger, green chilli, coriander, cashew nuts, kishmish and salt.
5. Stuff it into the boiled lauki pieces. Keep aside.
6. For masala- Heat 2 tbsp oil or ghee. Add laung, illaichi, dalchini and tej patta. Stir for a minute.
7. Add the prepared tomato paste. Stir for 3-4 minutes till thick and oil separates.
8. Add 1½ cups water. Boil. Simmer for 4-5 minutes till oil separates. Keep aside till serving time.
9. At serving time, saute lauki in a non stick pan in 1 tbsp oil, turning sides carefully to brown from all sides. Remove from pan.
10. Cut the lauki into ¾" thick round pieces. Transfer to a serving dish and pour the hot tomato gravy on top. Serve.

Moong Stuffed Tinda

Dal stuffed in round gourds.

Picture on page 103   *Serves 4*

500 gm (8-10) tinda - firm, medium sized
½ tsp salt
juice of 1 lemon, 2 tsp ginger paste
2 tsp dhania powder
½ tsp garam masala
¼ tsp red chilli powder
½ tsp haldi
a few tooth picks

FILLING
75 gm (½ cup) dhuli moong dal - soaked for 2 hours
½ cup (50 gm) grated paneer
1 tbsp desi ghee or oil
a pinch of hing (asafoetida)
½ tsp jeera (cumin seeds)

Filling Contd...

1 green chilli - finely chopped
½" piece ginger - finely chopped
½ tsp dhania powder
½ tsp red chilli powder
¼ tsp haldi
¾ tsp salt

1. Wash tindas. Scrape tindas and cut a thin slice from the top. Keep the thin slice (cap) aside. Scoop out tindas to make them hollow. Do not scoop to much.
2. Mix salt, lemon juice and ginger paste. Rub this on the inside and outside of the tindas.
3. Drain the soaked dal in a strainer.
4. Heat 1 tbsp ghee or oil in a heavy bottomed kadhai. Add a pinch of hing. Wait for 5-10 seconds.
5. Add jeera. Let jeera turn golden brown.
6. Reduce flame. Add ginger and green chilli. Mix.
7. Add dhania powder, red chilli powder and haldi.

Contd...

8. Add dal. Add salt to taste and cook covered on low flame for about 8-10 minutes or till dal is done. Sprinkle a little water in-between, if it sticks to the bottom of the kadhai.
9. Add paneer and mix well. Remove from fire.
10. Stuff the dal filling inside the scooped out tindas. Press well. Cover with the cap. Secure the cap with a toothpick.
11. Heat 3 tbsp oil in a kadhai. Add ½ tsp jeera and fry till golden.
12. Reduce flame and add 2 tsp dhania powder, ½ tsp garam masala, ¼ tsp red chilli powder and ½ tsp haldi.
13. Add the stuffed tindas one by one. Gently turn them lightly, to coat the oil all over. Cover and cook on low flame for 15-20 minutes till they feel soft when a knife is inserted in them. Keep turning sides in-between to brown the tindas evenly.

Tip: When buying tindas, remember to buy ones which have very fine hair on them, are green in colour and feel firm to touch.

Moong Stuffed Tinda: Recipe on page 100 ➢

Nita Mehta's BEST SELLERS (Vegetarian)

Cakes
& Chocolates

**The Art of
BAKING**

CHINESE
Vegetarian Cuisine

Mughlai
Vegetarian Khaana

SOUTH INDIAN

Taste of Punjab

HANDI TAWA KADHAI

ZERO OIL
Cookbook

BREAKFAST
Vegetarian Special

CHAWAL

JHATPAT KHAANA

Food for Children